I Have a Learning Disability and That's Okay

By Kacy Chambers

Copyright © Kacy C. Chambers 2021

All Rights Reserved.

No part of this book may be reproduced and transmitted in any form and by any means without the written permission of the author.

Photography and Illustrations © Kacy C. Chambers 2021

Editor: Carolyn M. Johnson

For more books by Kacy C. Chambers, visit her online at www.authorkacychambers.com

This book is dedicated to my incredible son Carter Chambers and everyone living with a Learning Disability.

I am different to you, but I look the same.

You cannot tell that I have a disability from my looks or my name.

Carter

Carter

Carter

Carter

Carter

Carter

A disability is something that makes it harder for people to do certain things.

Sometimes a person is born with it and sometimes they get it when they are older.

I can do a lot of the things that you can do.

Some things are hard for me, but they are easy for you.

One of those things is lacing a shoe.

It is hard for me to write, hold my pencil, or use scissors.

My work looks messy no matter how hard I try.

I want my paper to look nice like yours and this makes me want to cry.

It is not easy for me to learn things the way they are taught to you.

I hear the teacher talking but none of it makes sense.

This makes me feel like I am not as smart as other children.

I have trouble understanding what people are feeling when I am looking at their faces.

I do not know if you are happy, sad, or mad because to me all feelings look the same.

Jokes are hard for me to understand too.

When you tell a joke about me, I think you are being serious and that makes me mad.

I do not understand that it is a joke and that I should laugh.

I bump into things that seem to be in the way, and sometimes I fall over.

This is because I have trouble keeping my balance and making my body go straight.

Now that I have told you things that I do not like about my disability, let me tell you some ways it makes me feel unique.

Unique
means special

I know a lot of big words at a very young age.

This makes me a good reader which is great!

I am very kind.

This means if you treat me nicely, I will be your greatest buddy.

I ask a lot of questions.

This may sometimes be annoying.

However, the answers help me understand more as I'm growing.

You might have more questions and that is okay.

Maybe I can tell you more about it at lunch or when we go outside to play?

You should be kind to everyone, not just the people who look and act like you.

I hope we can be friends now. Let me know if this is true.

No matter what, I will hold my head up high each day.

I will look in the mirror at myself and say:

"I have a learning disability and that is okay."

www.ingramcontent.com/pod-product-compliance
Lightning Source LLC
Chambersburg PA
CBHW042255100526
44589CB00002B/33